Sunder
Quiz B

C000131410

101 Questions That Will Test Your Knowledge
Of This Prestigious Football Club

By Chris Carpenter
Published by Glowworm Press
7 Nuffield Way
Abingdon OX14 1RL

Sunderland Football Club

This book contains one hundred and one informative and entertaining trivia questions with multiple choice answers. Some questions are easy, some more demanding, and this book will test your knowledge of the Black Cats.

You will be quizzed on a wide range of topics associated with Sunderland AFC for you to test yourself, with questions on players, legends, managers, opponents, transfer deals, trophies, records, fixtures, songs and more, guaranteeing you both an educational experience and plenty of fun. With 101 questions, some easy, some more challenging, this book will test your knowledge and memory of the club's long and eventful history.

The **Sunderland Football Club** Quiz Book will provide the ultimate in entertainment for fans of all ages, and is a must-have for all loyal Sunderland fans.

2021/22 Season Edition

FOREWORD

When I was asked to write a foreword to this book I was deeply honoured.

I have known the author Chris Carpenter for many years and his knowledge of facts and figures is phenomenal.

His love for the North East and his huge talent for writing quiz books make him the ideal man to pay homage to my great love Sunderland A.F.C.

This book came about as a result of a challenge in a Lebanese restaurant of all places!

I do hope you enjoy the book.

Brian Kerr

Let's start with some relatively easy questions.

1. When was Sunderland founded?
        A. 1874
        B. 1876
        C. 1879

2. What is Sunderland's nickname?
        A. Black Cats
        B. Red Dogs
        C. Stripey Rabbits

3. Where does Sunderland play their home games?
        A. Stadium of Dreams
        B. Stadium of Hope
        C. Stadium of Light

4. What is the stadium's capacity?
        A. 43,000
        B. 46,000
        C. 49,000

5. Who or what is the club mascot?
        A. Samson and Delilah
        B. Stripey the Cat
        C. Terry Bytes

6. Who has made the most appearances for the club in total?
        A. Ned Doig
        B. Bobby Kerr
        C. Jimmy Montgomery

7. Who is the club's record goal scorer?
   A. Charlie Buchan
   B. Bobby Gurney
   C. Dave Halliday

8. Who is the fastest ever goal scorer for the club?
   A. Jimmy Gemmell
   B. Billy Hogg
   C. Ted Purdon

9. What song do the players run out to?
   A. Beginning of the Twist
   B. The Liquidator
   C. Insomnia

10. Which of these is a well known pub near the ground?
    A. The Sunderland Companions' Club
    B. The Sunderland Conservatives Club
    C. The Sunderland Contemptibles Club

OK, so here are the answers to the first ten questions. If you get eight or more right, you are doing very well so far, but don't get too cocky, as the questions do get harder.

A1. Sunderland was founded on the 17th October 1879.

A2. Sunderland's nickname is of course the Black Cats. There are other nicknames associated with the club including The Rokerites, The Roker Men, The Lads and Coal Cats.

A3. Sunderland plays their home games at the Stadium of Light. More questions to follow on the stadium later in the book.

A4. The current stadium capacity is 49,000. The design of the stadium is such that it can eventually be increased to just under 60,000.

A5. The club mascots are Samson and Delilah, and they are both black cats.

A6. Jimmy Montgomery has made the most appearances for the club. He played in 627 first-team matches from 1960 to 1977. Legend.

A7. Born in Silksworth, Bobby Gurney is Sunderland's record goal scorer with 228 goals, scored between 1926 and 1929.

A8. Ted Purdon scored just 10 seconds after kick off against Arsenal at Highbury, in only his second game for the club, back in January 1954.

A9. The players run out to the song 'Beginning of the Twist' as sung by The Futureheads.

A10. The Sunderland Companions' Club is a well known pub near the ground. Be prepared to queue for a pint though.

OK, let's have some ground related questions.

11. What is the club's record attendance?
   A. 73,992
   B. 74,554
   C. 75,118

12. Where did Sunderland play their home games before the Stadium of Light?
   A. Blundell Park
   B. Roker Park
   C. Upton Park

13. When did Sunderland move to the Stadium of Light?
   A. 1996
   B. 1997
   C. 1998

14. What is the name of the road the ground is on?
   A. Millennium Way
   B. Newcastle Road
   C. Shields Road

15. What stands at the entrance to the ground?
   A. An anvil
   B. A horseshoe
   C. A miner's lamp

16. How many England international matches have been held at the ground?
   A. 1
   B. 2

C. 3

17. In which stand do the away fans sit?
    A. East Stand
    B. North Stand
    C. South Stand

18. What is the size of the pitch?
    A. 110x72m
    B. 105x68m
    C. 105x62m

19. Which of these groups have played a concert at the Stadium of Light?
    A. Blur
    B. Take That
    C. Travis

20. What is Sunderland's training ground called?
    A. The Academy of Light
    B. Charlie Hurley Centre
    C. The Institute of Excellence

Here are the answers to the last set of questions.

A11. Sunderland's record home attendance is 75,118; for an FA Cup match against Derby County on 8th March 1933.

A12. Sunderland played at Roker Park for 99 years. People who love football throughout the world know the phrase "The Roker Roar".

A13. The Stadium of Light was opened by Price Andrew on 30th July 1997. This was followed by the club playing their first game - a friendly against Ajax on the same day.

A14. The official address of the Stadium is Millennium Way, Sunderland SR5 1SU.

A15. A Davy lamp monument stands at the entrance to the ground by the ticket office, to reflect the coal mining industry that brought prosperity to the town. The name "Stadium of Light" was chosen as an ever lasting tribute to the region's mine workers that emerged every working day from the darkness underground and into the light. The ground was built on the site of the old Wearmouth Colliery pit.

A16. The ground has hosted three England internationals, a friendly on 10th October 1999 which resulted in a 2-1 victory over Belgium; on 2nd April 2003 a Euro 2004 qualifying game against Turkey, which England won 2-0; and more recently a friendly on 27th May 2016, a friendly against Australia which England won 2-1.

A17. Away fans sit in the upper tier of the North Stand.

A18. The size of the pitch is 105 metres long by 68 metres wide. If you prefer imperial measurements then it is 115 yards long and 75 yards wide.

A19. Take That have performed twice at the stadium. They performed in 2009 and also in 2011. Other acts that have performed at the Stadium include Beyonce, Coldplay, Kings of Leon, Oasis and Rihanna.

A20. The Academy of Light is the name of the UEFA five star certified training facilities for the club. It is located in Cleadon, just north of the city centre. It opened in March 2003 replacing the ageing Charlie Hurley Centre.

Here is the next set of questions.

21. What is the club's record win in any
    competition?
    A. 12-0
    B. 14-0
    C. 23-0

22. Who did they beat?
    A. Castletown
    B. Chatham
    C. Fairfield

23. In which season?
    A. 1883/84
    B. 1895/96
    C. 1907/08

24. What is the highest number of goals that
    Sunderland has scored in a league season?
    A. 101
    B. 105
    C. 109

25. What is the fewest number of goals that
    Sunderland has conceded in a league season?
    A. 23
    B. 26
    C. 29

26. What is the club's record defeat?
    A. 0-7
    B. 1-8

C. 0-8

27. Who was the club's record defeat against?
    A. Sheffield Wednesday
    B. Watford
    C. West Ham United

28. Who has made the most *League* appearances for the club?
    A. Michael Gray
    B. George Holley
    C. Jim Montgomery

29. Who has scored the most hat tricks for Sunderland in the Premier League?
    A. Darren Bent
    B. Adam Johnson
    C. Kevin Phillips

30. How many games have Sunderland played in European football?
    A. 4
    B. 6
    C. 8

Here are the answers to the last set of questions.

A21. The club's record win in any competition is 23-0.

A22. The club beat Castletown 23-0. It was an official match so it therefore goes into the record books.

A23. The match took place on 20th December 1884, so it was the 1883/84 season.

A24. Sunderland scored 109 goals in 42 matches in the First Division in the 1955/56 season.

A25. Sunderland conceded just 26 goals in 34 matches in the First Division in the 1900/01 season.

A26. The club's record defeat in any competition is 0-8.

A27. All three is the right answer. Sunderland lost 8-0 to Sheffield Wednesday on 26th December 1911; West Ham United on 19th October 1968; and to Watford on 25th September 1982, all by the same score. The club also shamefully lost 8-0 to Southampton, in the Premier League era; on the 18th October 2014.

A28. Jimmy Montgomery holds the record for the most league appearances for the club, with 537 league appearances in total. Legend.

A29. Kevin Phillips has scored the most hat tricks for Sunderland in the Premier League - two. In his time at the club he scored 130 goals in 235 matches.

A30. The club has somewhat surprisingly only played four games in European football, all in the European Cup Winners Cup in the 1973/74 season.

Now we move onto questions about some of the club's trophies.

31. How many times have Sunderland won the League?
    A. 2
    B. 4
    C. 6

32. How many times have Sunderland won the FA Cup?
    A. 0
    B. 1
    C. 2

33. How many times have Sunderland won the League Cup?
    A. 0
    B. 1
    C. 2

34. When did the club win their first league title?
    A. 1890/91
    B. 1891/92
    C. 1892/93

35. Who was the *last* captain to lift the First Division League trophy?
    A. Stan Anderson
    B. Raich Carter
    C. Bobby Gurney

36. When did the club win their first FA Cup?

A. 1927
B. 1937
C. 1947

37. Who did they beat in the final?
    A. Derby County
    B. Ipswich Town
    C. Preston North End

38. When did the club win their last FA Cup?
    A. 1971
    B. 1973
    C. 1975

39. Who did they beat in the final?
    A. Leicester City
    B. Leeds United
    C. Liverpool

40. Who was the *last* captain to lift the FA Cup?
    A. Vic Halom
    B. Bobby Kerr
    C. Jim Montgomery

Here are the answers to the last block of questions.

A31. Sunderland have won the league 6 times in total. (1891/92, 1892/93, 1894/95, 1901/02, 1912/13, 1935/36)

A32. Sunderland have won the FA Cup twice. (1937 and 1973)

A33. Sunderland have never won the League Cup. However they were finalists in 1985 and 2014.

A34. Sunderland won their first League title in 1891/92.

A35. Raich Carter was the last captain to lift the First Division League trophy. He lifted the trophy at the end of the 1935/36 season.

A36. Sunderland won their first FA Cup in 1937.

A37. Sunderland defeated Preston North End 3-1 at Wembley Stadium on the 1st May 1937, with goals from Bobby Gurney, Raich Carter and Eddie Burbanks.

A38. Sunderland won their last FA Cup in 1973.

A39. Sunderland defeated hot favourites Leeds United 1-0 on 5th May 1973 at Wembley Stadium. For everyone who was there, it will never be forgotten.

A40. Bobby Kerr was the captain who last lifted the FA Cup that glorious Spring day.

I hope you're having fun, and getting most of the answers right.

41. What is the record transfer fee paid?
    A. £12.8 million
    B. £13.8 million
    C. £14.8 million

42. Who was the record transfer fee paid for?
    A. Steven Fletcher
    B. Asamoah Gyan
    C. Didier N'Dong

43. What is the record transfer fee received?
    A. £26 million
    B. £28 million
    C. £30 million

44. Who was the record transfer fee received for?
    A. Darren Bent
    B. Simon Mignolet
    C. Jordan Pickford

45. Who was the first Sunderland player to play for England?
    A. Arthur Bridgett
    B. Billy Hogg
    C. Thomas Porteous

46. Who has won the most international caps whilst a Sunderland player?
    A. Charlie Hurley
    B. Kenwyne Jones

C. Kevin Kilbane

47. Who among the following has scored the most international goals whilst a Sunderland player?
    A. Charlie Buchan
    B. Raich Carter
    C. George Holley

48. Who is the youngest player ever to represent the club?
    A. Derek Forster
    B. Michael Gray
    C. Dave Halliday

49. Who scored the first league hat trick for the club?
    A. John Campbell
    B. James Gillespie
    C. John Scott

50. Who is the oldest player ever to represent the club?
    A. George Baddeley
    B. Joe Carter
    C. Tommy Urwin

Here are the answers to the last set of questions.

A41. In 2016, Sunderland paid 16 million Euros, the equivalent of £13.8 million, for a player from Gabon, which is the club's record transfer.

A42. The fee was paid to French club Lorient for Didier N'Dong on 31st August 2016.

A43. The record transfer fee received by Sunderland is £30 million.

A44. The fee was received from Everton for goalkeeper Jordan Pickford on 1st July 2017.

A45. Thomas Porteous was the first Sunderland player to play for England. He made his one and only appearance for his country, against Wales on 7th March 1891.

A46. Charlie Hurley won 36 caps for the Republic of Ireland while he was at Sunderland, which is the highest number of caps by anyone whilst at the club.

A47. George Holley scored the most international goals whilst a Sunderland player, netting eight times in ten appearances between 1909 and 1912.

A48. Derek Forster is the youngest player ever to represent the club. He made his first team appearance at the age of 15 years, 185 days against Leicester City on 22nd August 1964.

A49. John Campbell scored the first hat trick for the club. He scored it against Bolton in the 1890/91 season.

A50. Tommy Urwin is the oldest player ever to represent the club, turning out against Preston North End on 22nd April 1935 aged 39 years and 76 days.

I hope you're learning some new facts about the club, and here is the next set of questions.

51. Who was known as The Clown Prince of Soccer?
    A. Jozy Altidore
    B. Bryan "Pop" Robson
    C. Len Shackleton

52. Who is the club's longest serving manager of all time?
    A. Alan Brown
    B. Bob Kyle
    C. Alex Mackie

53. Who is the club's longest serving post-war manager?
    A. Alan Brown
    B. Alan Durban
    C. Bob Stokoe

54. What is the name of the Sunderland match day programme?
    A. Black Cat News
    B. Red and White
    C. The Wearside Roar

55. What is the name of the club's official twitter account?
    A. @officialsunderland
    B. @sunderland
    C. @sunderlandafc

56. Which of these is a Sunderland fanzine?

A. The Last Bus to Rolfe
B. A Love Supreme
C. The Roar

57. What animal is on the club crest?
    A. Leopard
    B. Lion
    C. Tiger

58. What is the club's motto?
    A. Consectatio Excellentiae
    B. Labor omnia vincit
    C. Nil Satis Nisi Optimum

59. Who is considered as Sunderland's main rivals?
    A. Darlington
    B. Middlesbrough
    C. Newcastle United

60. Which of the following is a popular Sunderland chant?
    A. Ha'Way The Lads
    B. Niall Quinn's Disco Pants
    C. The Wearside Races

Here are the answers to the last set of questions.

A51. Len Shackleton who played 348 games for Sunderland from 1948 to 1957 was known as "The Crown Prince" as he was one of the games' original entertainers. He was also Sunderland's oldest ever goal scorer, scoring at the age of 32 years and 182 days.

A52. Bob Kyle is the club's longest serving manager of all time. He was in charge for 803 games from August 1905 to March 1928. It's a record that is unlikely to be broken.

A53. Alan Brown is the club's longest serving post war manager. He served from 1957 to 1964 and then again from 1968 to 1972 managing a total of 551 matches.

A54. The name of the Sunderland match day programme is Red and White.

A55. @SunderlandAFC is the official twitter account of the club. It tweets multiple times a day, and it has almost a million followers.

A56. A Love Supreme is perhaps the best known Sunderland fanzine. It also has a very popular website. Let's not forget It's The Hope I Can't Stand though.

A57. Supporting either side of the club crest are two majestic lions.

A58. The Latin motto of Sunderland is 'Consectatio Excellentiae'. It means 'In pursuit of excellence' in English.

A59. Easy question. Newcastle United is considered as Sunderland's main rival. Sunderland contests the Tyne-Wear derby with them.

A60. "Ha'way The Lads" is a chant Sunderland fans sing with gusto home and away.

Let's give you some easier questions.

61. What is the traditional colour of the home shirt?
    A. Blue and white stripes
    B. Red and white stripes
    C. Red and black stripes

62. What is the traditional colour of the away shirt?
    A. Blue
    B. Pink
    C. Yellow

63. Who is the current club shirt sponsor?
    A. Gas Analysis Sensing Group
    B. Global Audit Steering Group
    C. Great Annual Savings Group

64. Who was the first club shirt sponsor?
    A. Cowie's
    B. Reg Vardy
    C. Vaux Breweries

65. Which of these have once sponsored the club?
    A. Boylesports
    B. JD Sports
    C. Sports Direct

66. Who currently owns the club?
    A. Stewart Donald
    B. Kyril Louis-Dreyfus
    C. Ellis Short

67. Who was the club's first foreign signing?

A. James Dalton
B. Don Kitchenbrand
C. Dariusz Kubicki

68. Who was the club's first black player?
A. Reuben Agbola
B. Roly Gregoire
C. Billy Troughear

69. Who was the leading scorer for the 2020/21 season?
A. Chris Maguire
B. Aiden McGeady
C. Charlie Wyke

70. What position did the club finish at the end of the 2020/21 season?
A. 4th
B. 5th
C. 6th

Here are the answers to the last ten questions.

A61. The traditional colour of the home shirt is of course red and white stripes.

A62. The traditional colour of the away shirt is a tricky one, as many colours have been used. However, historically the club has worn blue (in various shades, and patterns) as its change kit more than any other colour.

A63. Seaham based Great Annual Savings Group are the current shirt sponsor.

A64. Cowie's, the business group of then chairman Tom Cowie, was the first shirt sponsor of Sunderland, back in 1983.

A65. Boylesports sponsored the club from 2007 to 2010.

A66. Tycoon Kyril Louis-Dreyfus is the current owner of the club. He became owner and took over the role as club chairman in February 2021.

A67. James Dalton was Sunderland's first foreign signing; he joined the team in 1893 and played just 3 games before moving back to Canada.

A68. Roly Gregoire was the club's first black player, making his debut on 2nd January 1978, and going on to play just nine games before retiring in 1980 due to injury.

A69. The leading goal scorer for the 2020/21 season was Charlie Wyke, who scored 31 goals in total during the season, including 25 in the league.

A70. Sunderland finished 4th in League One at the end of the 2020/21 season.

Here is the next batch of ten carefully chosen questions.

71. Which English forward scored in the first 33 spot kicks that he took for Sunderland after joining the club in 1908?
    A. Charlie Buchan
    B. Billy Hogg
    C. Jackie Mordue

72. Who scored the only goal of the game in the 1973 FA Cup Final?
    A. Vic Halom
    B. Billy Hughes
    C. Ian Porterfield

73. Which Scottish forward was nicknamed "Cannonball"?
    A. Charlie Fleming
    B. James Connor
    C. Nicky Sharkey

74. Who holds the record for the most goals scored in a season for the club?
    A. Charlie Buchan
    B. Bobby Gurney
    C. Dave Halliday

75. Where was Will Grigg born?
    A. England
    B. Northern Ireland
    C. Scotland

76. Who was the first full time manager of the club?
    A. Robert Campbell
    B. Alex Mackie
    C. Tom Watson

77. Who started the 2021/2022 season as manager?
    A. Lee Johnson
    B. Phil Parkinson
    C. Jack Ross

78. How many FA Cup goals did Bobby Gurney score for the club?
    A. 21
    B. 23
    C. 25

79. Who was the manager of the FA Cup winning side of 1973?
    A. Bob Hope
    B. Bill Murray
    C. Bob Stokoe

80. Where was club legend Charlie Hurley born?
    A. England
    B. Ireland
    C. Scotland

Here are the answers to the last set of questions.

A71. Jackie Mordue scored in the first 33 spot kicks that he took for Sunderland after joining the club in 1908.

A72. Ian Porterfield scored the only goal of the 1973 FA Cup Final, in the 31st minute. I have seen that goal hundreds of times, and I can still see it now!

A73. Charlie Fleming was nicknamed "Cannonball".

A74. With 43 goals in the 1928/29 season, Dave Halliday holds the record for the most goals scored in a season for the club.

A75. Although Will Grigg plays for Northern Ireland, he was born in Solihull, Birmingham.

A76. Tom Watson was the first full time manager of the club. He managed 191 matches for the club from August 1888 to August 1896.

A77. Lee Johnson started the 2021/22 season as manager, having been appointed to the role in December 2020.

A78. Bobby Gurney scored 23 FA Cup goals for the club.

A79. Bob Stokoe was of course the manager of the 1973 FA Cup winning side.

A80. Tough tackling defender Charlie Hurley was born in Cork in Ireland. Talk to any old timer, and they will tell you he is the greatest player the club has ever had.

Here is the next set of questions, let's hope you get most of them right.

81. Who currently supplies kit to the first team?
    A. Adidas
    B. Nike
    C. Umbro

82. In which country was Lynden Gooch born?
    A. Canada
    B. Mexico
    C. USA

83. In 1979, who was voted as Sunderland's Player of the Century?
    A. Charlie Buchan
    B. Dave Halliday
    C. Charlie Hurley

84. Which Scottish forward scored 12 hat tricks and a total of 162 goals for the club?
    A. Johnny Campbell
    B. Dave Halliday
    C. Jimmy Millar

85. When was Sunderland relegated from the First Division for the first time?
    A. 1950
    B. 1954
    C. 1958

86. Who scored five goals for the club against Norwich in a 7-1 win in March 1963?

A. Johnny Crossan
B. George Mulhall
C. Nicky Sharkey

87. Which club did Sunderland defeat to earn the title of "Champions of the World" in 1895?
    A. Aberdeen
    B. Heart of Midlothian
    C. Hibernian

88. Who was the club's first professional captain?
    A. Ned Doig
    B. Will Gibson
    C. James McMillan

89. Which MLS side did the club enter into a commercial partnership with in 2014?
    A. DC United
    B. LA Galaxy
    C. New York Red Bulls

90. When did Sunderland qualify for the UEFA Cup Winners' Cup?
    A. 1970
    B. 1973
    C. 1976

Here are the answers to the last set of questions.

A81. The kit is currently supplied by Nike, who took over from Adidas in time for the 2020/21 season.

A82. Winger Lynden Jack Gooch was born in California, USA.

A83. On the occasion of the club's centenary in 1979, Hurley was named the Black Cats' "Player of The Century".

A84. Dave Halliday scored 12 hat tricks and a total of 162 goals for the club.

A85. Sunderland were relegated from the First Division for the first time in 1958.

A86. Nicky Sharkey scored five goals for the club against Norwich in a 7-1 win in March 1963.

A87. Sunderland earned the title of "Champions of the World" by defeating the champions of the Scottish League, Heart of Midlothian 5-3 in 1895. The match was described as 'Championship of the world title match'.

A88. James McMillan was the club's first professional captain.

A89. In August 2014 the club announced a commercial partnership with Washington DC based MLS side DC United.

A90. By virtue of winning the FA Cup in 1973, Sunderland qualified for the UEFA Cup Winners' Cup for the 1973/74 season.

Here is the final set of questions. Enjoy!

91. What is the official website address?
    A. safc.com
    B. sunderland.com
    C. sunderlandfc.com

92. How many seasons have Sunderland had in the Premier League?
    A. 14
    B. 15
    C. 16

93. What is the best finish for the club in the Premier League?
    A. 6th
    B. 7th
    C. 8th

94. Who is the highest goal scorer of the club in the Premier League era?
    A. Jermain Defoe
    B. Kevin Phillips
    C. Niall Quinn

95. Who made his debut for the club against Chelsea at the age of 18 years and 137 days in November 2008?
    A. Jordan Henderson
    B. Louis Laing
    C. Martyn Waghorn

96. What was Sunderland AFC called when the club was formed?
   A. Sunderland FC
   B. Sunderland and District Teachers' AFC
   C. Sunderland Strollers

97. What did former Sunderland chairman Bob Murray describe the club as?
   A. Bank of England Club
   B. Club of All Talents
   C. Labour Club

98. Who is the club captain for the 2021/2022 season?
   A. Corry Evans
   B. Tom Flanagan
   C. Denver Hume

99. What is the biggest transfer fee received by the club for a player produced by the Sunderland Academy?
   A. £20 million
   B. £25 million
   C. £30 million

100. Where did Sunderland get its nickname from?
   A. A brand of cigarettes
   B. A stray black cat
   C. Napoleonic Wars

101. Whose statue is present outside the ground?
    A. Sam Allardyce
    B. Niall Quinn
    C. Bob Stokoe

Here are the answers to the last set of questions.

A91. safc.com is the official website address.

A92. 2016/17 was the 16th season Sunderland played in the Premier League. Hopefully the club will be back there soon.

A93. The club finished 7th in the Premier League in both the 1999/2000 and 2000/01 seasons, which is their best finish in the Premier League era.

A94. With 61 Premier League goals, Kevin Phillips is the highest goal scorer for the club in the Premier League.

A95. Jordan Henderson made his debut for the club against Chelsea at the age of 18 years and 137 days in November 2008.

A96. Sunderland was founded on the 17th October 1879 as Sunderland and District Teachers AFC.

A97. Former Sunderland chairman Bob Murray described the club as the "Labour Club". Official government statistics show that the club has many fans with a left wing political persuasion.

A98. Corry Evans is the club captain for the 2021/22 season.

A99. In June 2017 a fee of £25 million, with add-ons rising to £30 million was received from Everton for the transfer of Jordan Pickford, a product of the Sunderland Academy. This eclipsed the previous record of £11 million paid by Liverpool for Jordan Henderson in June 2011. Pickford joined the Academy at just eight years old.

A100. In January 1909 Sunderland were going through a lean spell. A stray black cat wandered into the dressing room prior to a 3-1 victory over Bury which led to the feline mascot being adopted by the players. Whether the victory was a co-incidence or due to the lucky black cat, no-one will ever know; but to this day the club is known as the Black Cats.

A101. There is a wonderful statue of Bob Stokoe with his arms aloft celebrating the 1973 FA Cup Final victory outside the ground.

That's a great one to finish with. I hope you enjoyed this book, and I hope you got most of the answers right. I also hope you learnt a few new things about the club

If you see anything wrong, or have a general comment, please visit the glowwormpress.com website.

Thanks for reading, and if you did enjoy the book, would you please leave a positive review on Amazon.

Ha'way The Lads.

Printed in Great Britain
by Amazon